It's OK to Work Hard
and Make It Happen!

By: Kenny Kiskis

ISBN 979-8-990-2790-6-3

©2024 Kenny Kiskis

It's OK to Work Hard and Make It Happen!

In every student, where possibilities shine,
This book only has your happiness in mind.
With each page turned, a new path appears,
Leading to futures and possible careers.

Study very hard, with all your might,
For knowledge is power, a guiding light.
In these pages lie treasures untold,
Opportunities waiting for you to behold.

So explore each page of this book,
At the future before you, take a good look.
With this book as your trusted friend,
Your journey to success has no end.

With effort and heart, you'll pave the way,
To a successful future, come what may.
With devotion and dedication, you will find,
The perfect career, that's one of a kind.

So work hard, aim high, and don't delay,
This book will guide you on your way.

IT'S OK TO WORK HARD IN SCHOOL

Do you know why it's super important to work hard in school?

Good Grades: When you pay attention in class and finish your homework on time, you're more likely to get good grades. That means you'll do really well on tests and quizzes!

Understanding Stuff: When you pay attention in class and finish your homework, you'll understand what your teacher is talking about much better. That makes learning easier and more fun!

Being Responsible: Finishing your homework shows that you're responsible. It's like saying, "I'm in charge of my own learning!" Plus, it helps you learn to manage your time better.

Feeling Confident: When you do well in school, it feels amazing! You start believing in yourself more and know you can handle tough stuff.

Getting Ready for the Future: All the hard work you do now sets you up for success later on. Whether it's going to college or chasing your dream job, the skills you learn now will help you get there.

So, keep up the good work! Working hard in school now will pay off big time in the future. You got this!

ARCHITECTS
design buildings like hotels, schools, office spaces and hospitals that are safe, functional and aesthetically pleasing.

ARTISTS
are creative storytellers who use their talents to express themselves in various ways. They paint vivid pictures, sculpt statues, write stories, compose beautiful music, and perform breathtaking dances. Each artist has their own unique style and vision.

ATHLETES
demonstrate dedication, discipline, and teamwork, serving as role models for young people.

CHEFS

Nourish and deilight us with their delicious food. They use recipes and ingredients to cook tasty meals, using techniques like chopping, grilling, and sautéing.

Chefs work in restaurants, hotels, or even on TV shows

CHILDCARE PROVIDERS care for and nurture young children while supporting families and providing early social and child developmental skills.

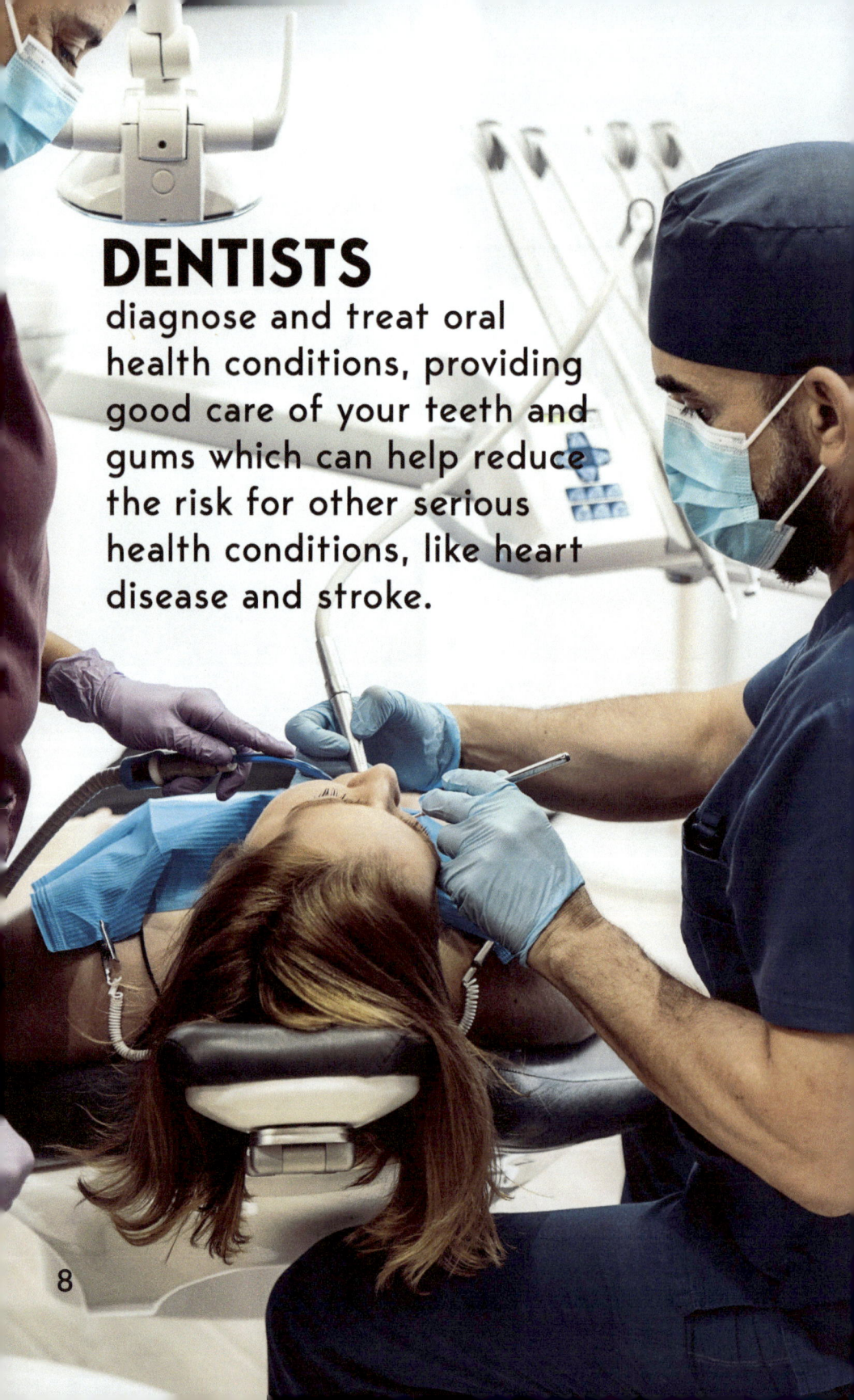

DENTISTS
diagnose and treat oral health conditions, providing good care of your teeth and gums which can help reduce the risk for other serious health conditions, like heart disease and stroke.

DESIGNERS

Graphic Designers, Fashion Designers & Interior Designers

Designers are super creative. They're like artists, but instead of painting on a canvas, they use their imagination to make things like logos, dresses, or even the layout of a room look cool and unique. They figure out how to make something not only look good but also work well.

DOCTORS
work tirelessly to keep people healthy and save lives. They help us stay healthy and treat us when we're sick or hurt.

EMERGENCY MEDICAL TECHNICIANS (EMTs) provide critical medical care in emergencies, including saving lives, often under challenging conditions.

IT'S OK TO BE CONSIDERATE AND KIND TO OTHER PEOPLE

Have you ever wondered why it's super important to be nice and respectful to others?

First off, when you're friendly and kind to people, you build really good relationships. Think about it like making awesome friends! When you get along with others, it makes everything easier and more fun.

Plus, being respectful and friendly helps you learn how to talk to people. You know, like saying "please" and "thank you" and listening when someone else is talking. These are called communication skills, and they're super important no matter what job you want to do when you grow up.

Remember, whether you're a doctor, a teacher, or even an astronaut, you'll need to work with other people. And when you're nice and can talk to people well, it makes everything go smoothly.

So, be kind—it'll help you in whatever you choose to do now and in the future!

ENGINEERS use math, science and creative thinking to solve problems and make things that help make our lives easier. They design buildings, roads, bridges, cars, computers, and even rollercoasters!

FIRE FIGHTERS risk their lives to protect people and property from fires and other emergency situations.

HUMANITARIAN WORKERS
provide aid and assistance to people affected by financial hardship, disasters and conflicts.

INTERNET TECHNOLOGY (IT) PROFESSIONALS

maintain and secure technology systems, enabling communication and innovation.

JOURNALISTS
write articles or make videos about things happening in our town, country, or even around the globe. They talk to people, go to events, and do research to find out what's going on. Then, they share the news with everyone so we can all stay informed!

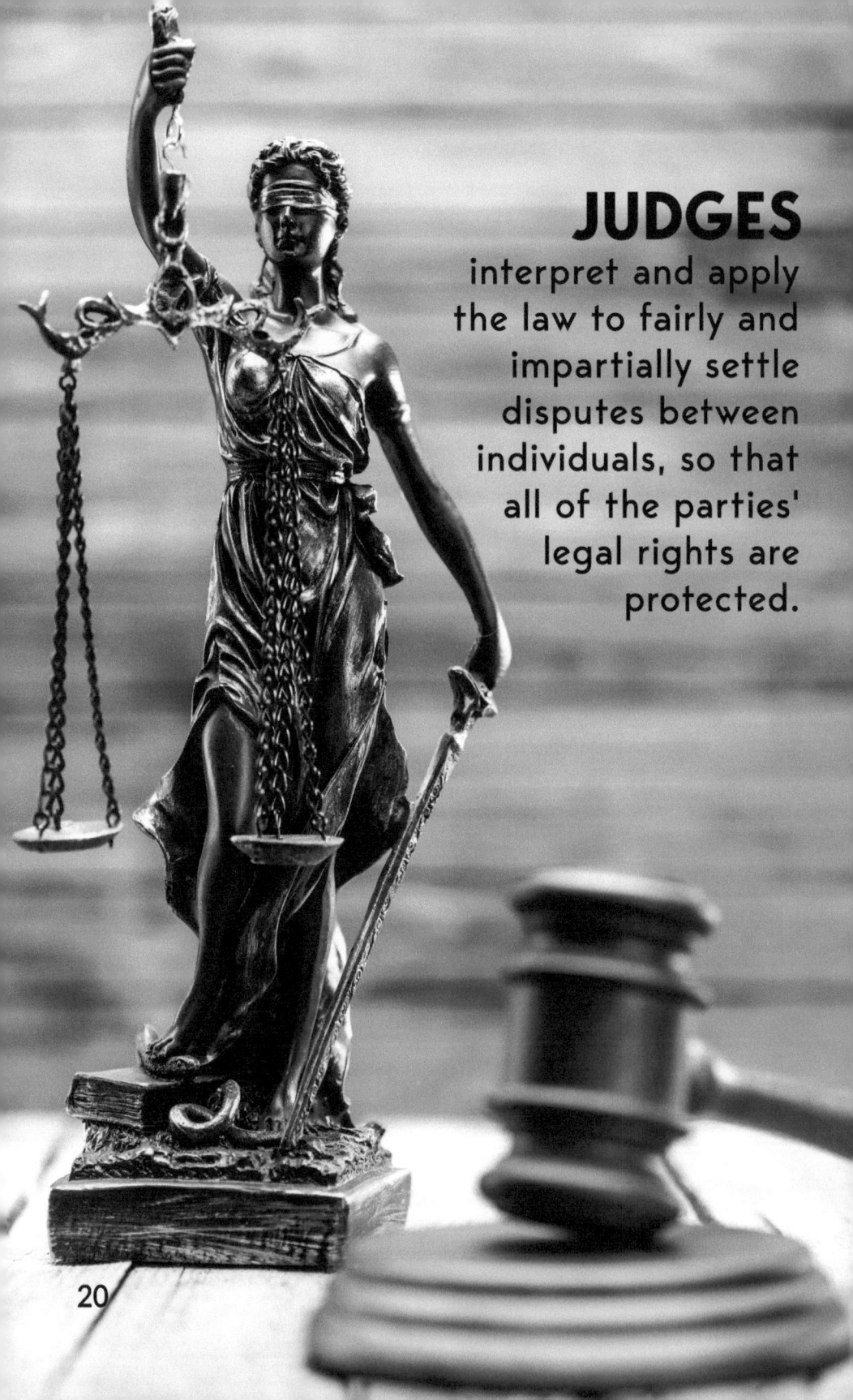

JUDGES interpret and apply the law to fairly and impartially settle disputes between individuals, so that all of the parties' legal rights are protected.

LAWYERS
uphold justice and defend the rights of individuals and communities.

IT'S OK TO ACT RESPECTFUL

Here's a few ways how to show respect to your parents, teachers and people in charge.

Listen and follow instructions: Pay attention when your parents or teachers speak to you, and try your best to do what they ask.

Use polite language: Always use words like "please" and "thank you" when talking to your parents, teachers, or any adults.

Be helpful: Offer to help with tasks around the house without being asked, like setting the table or taking out the trash.

Be honest: Always tell the truth, even if you're scared of getting into trouble. Your parents and teachers will appreciate your honesty.

Appreciate their efforts: Let your parents know you're grateful for what they do for you, whether it's making dinner or helping with homework.

Follow rules: Understand that rules are there to keep you safe and help you learn. Respect and obey them, even if you don't always agree.

Be considerate: Think about how your actions might affect others. Avoid yelling, slamming doors, or being disrespectful when you're upset.

Showing respect means being kind, polite, and considerate towards your parents and authority figures. It's about treating them the way you want to be treated.

LIBRARIANS
are expert guides in the world of books and information. They organize books, magazines, and digital resources so you can easily discover what interests you. They encourage a love of reading and learning.

MENTAL HEALTH PROFESSIONALS

talk to people about their feelings and problems, offer advice and support, and sometimes provide therapy or counseling to help them feel better. They teach ways to deal with stress or anxiety and work with other professionals to come up with plans to improve mental well-being.

MUSIC PRODUCER

helps artists bring their ideas to life, guiding singers and musicians to express themselves in the best way possible.

They're the ones who take a song from just an idea to a finished masterpiece.

NURSES

work tirelessly to provide compassionate care and support to patients in need. They provide a wide range of medical services, including administering medications, monitoring patients' conditions, and assisting with treatments and procedures.

NUTRITIONISTS

teach us about good foods to eat and how much we should have. By doing this, they keep us strong and help prevent sickness. They also work to make sure everyone has enough healthy food to eat.

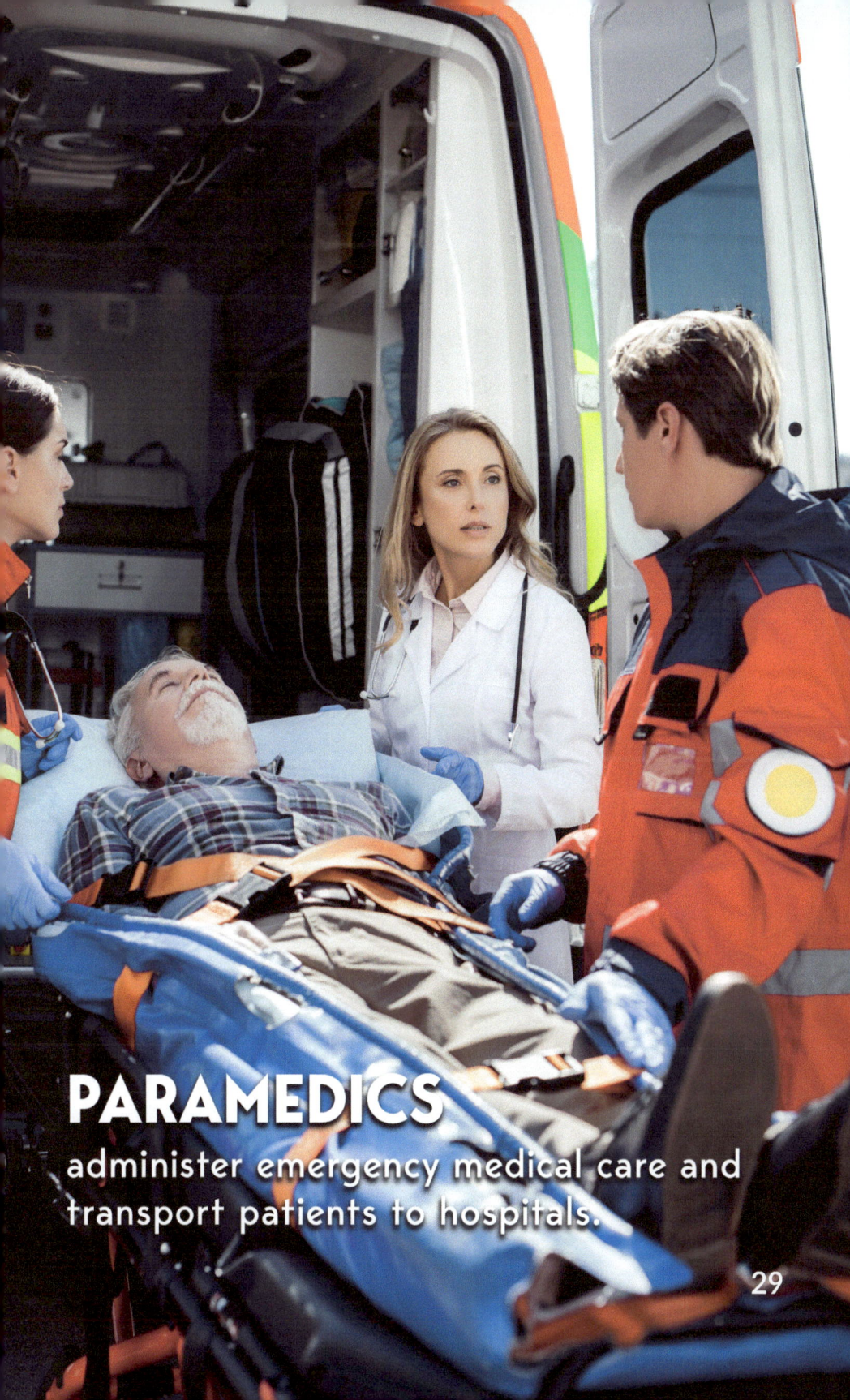

PARAMEDICS
administer emergency medical care and transport patients to hospitals.

PHARMACISTS
dispense medication and offer advice on its proper use, promoting health and well-being.

POLICE OFFICERS
work to keep people safe by enforcing laws, responding to emergencies, and helping during accidents or crimes. They patrol neighborhoods, investigate incidents, and make arrests when needed. They also work to prevent crime by educating the public and building positive relationships with communities.

IT'S OK TO TRY NEW THINGS

Here's why it's important to try out a lot of different subjects and activities in school!

First off, trying out different things helps you figure out what you're passionate about and what you excel at. It's the perfect way to find out more about yourself by exploring other interests and talents.

Also, trying new activities teaches you valuable skills that you can use throughout your life. Whether it's teamwork, problem-solving, or creativity, these skills are like building blocks that help you succeed in school and beyond.

And yes, trying new things isn't always easy. You might face challenges and setbacks along the way. But working through these obstacles teaches you inner strength and how to bounce back from challenges which strengthens your character.

Lastly, exploring many other interests opens up a world of opportunities for your future. It might lead you to discover career paths you never considered or hobbies that you really like and give you joy.

So, take that adventure of trying new things in school. It's not just about having fun—it's about growing as an individual and preparing yourself for the exciting journey ahead.

PILOTS

use their technical abilities and strong communication skills to navigate and operate aircraft safely, all while prioritizing the well-being and efficient transportation of passengers, cargo, or both

SCIENTISTS

expand our knowledge of the world and develop solutions to complex problems. They discover new things and research how things work which can help advance our quality of life.

SOCIAL WORKERS

are helpers who support people and families facing tough times. They listen to their problems, offer advice and resources, and help them find solutions to improve their lives.

TEACHERS educate and shape young minds, playing a crucial role in their development.

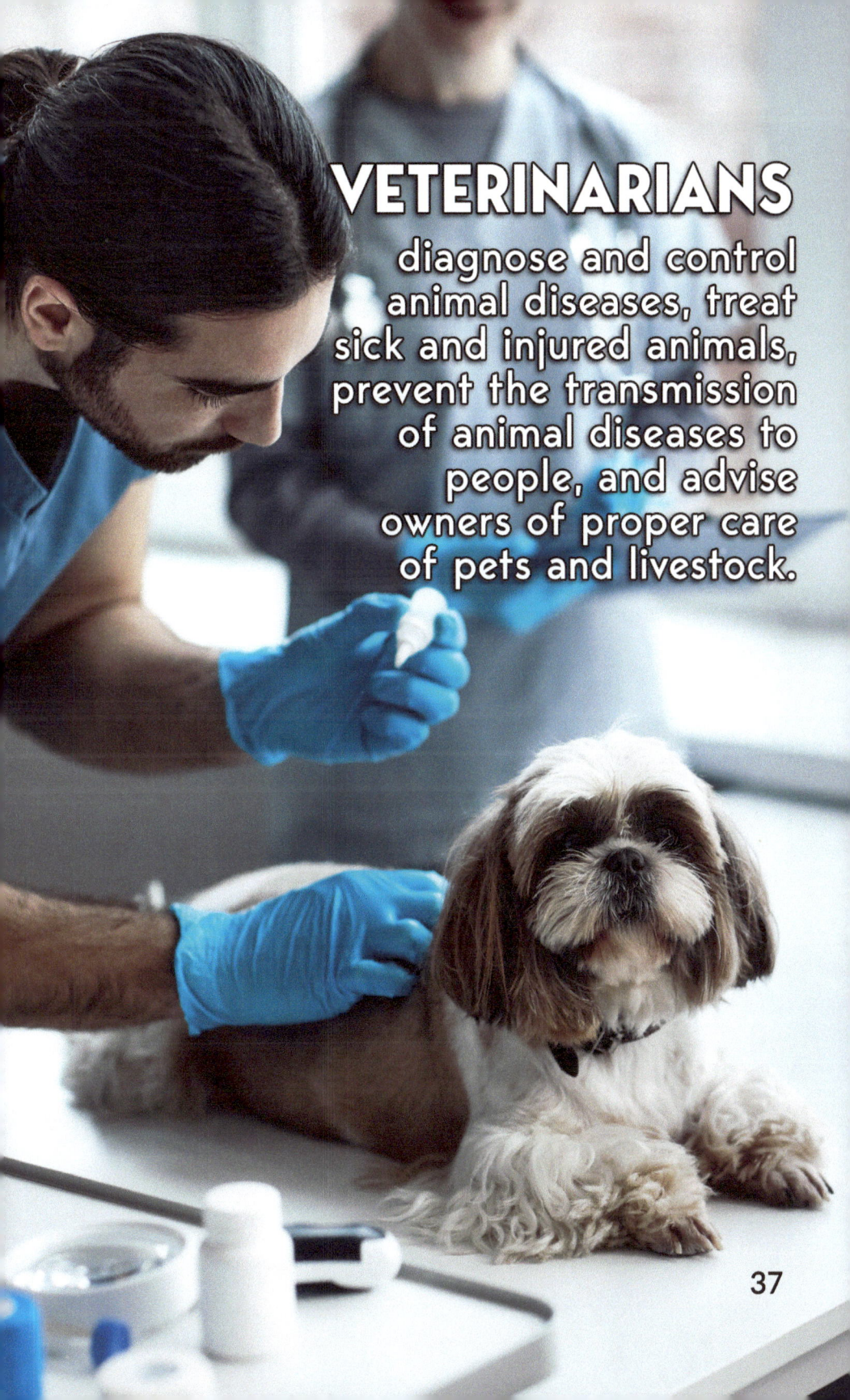

VETERINARIANS

diagnose and control animal diseases, treat sick and injured animals, prevent the transmission of animal diseases to people, and advise owners of proper care of pets and livestock.

ZOOLOGISTS

are scientists who study animals and their habitats. They research animal behavior, ecosystems, and conservation needs. They play a critical role in protecting endangered species and preserving the delicate balance of nature.

Kenny Kiskis is a multifaceted individual, best known as the author of **"Word's Don't Stick**," a straight-forward guide empowering children to overcome name-calling and cultivate resilience. Through his work, Kiskis offers invaluable insights into fostering tough-love development in children.

His passion for empowering parents led him to write **"It's OK to say Go Play**," a tough love guide that emphasizes the importance of independent play in children's cognitive growth. Kiskis firmly believes in the power of play for nurturing creativity and problem-solving skills in young minds.

Beyond his contributions to parenting literature, Kenny Kiskis is an entrepreneur and business owner. He founded PrivacyShields.com, a company dedicated to improving student test scores, as well as SearchBarTees.com, which offers customized hilarious apparel.

With a blend of entrepreneurial spirit and a commitment to fostering healthy child development, Kenny Kiskis continues to make a meaningful impact in both the business and parenting realm

"It's OK to Work Hard and Make It Happen!", Kiskis's third book is an A-to-Z career guide packed with vibrant pictures and individual job descriptions. From doctors healing patients to engineers building bridges, each page sparks imagination and ambition.

This book not only inspires young teens to explore future career paths but also includes valuable advice about trying new things, being respectful to others and working hard in school.

Kenny's book serves not only as a career guide, but also a reminder that with dedication and effort, the possibilities are endless!

NOTES